ZOE
GETS HER
ZOOM BACK

KATHY V. KUZMA

AuthorHouse™
1663 Liberty Drive
Bloomington, IN 47403
www.authorhouse.com
Phone: 833-262-8899

Because of the dynamic nature of the Internet, any web addresses or links contained in this book may have changed since publication and may no longer be valid. The views expressed in this work are solely those of the author and do not necessarily reflect the views of the publisher, and the publisher hereby disclaims any responsibility for them.

Any people depicted in stock imagery provided by Getty Images are models, and such images are being used for illustrative purposes only.
Certain stock imagery © Getty Images.

This book is printed on acid-free paper.

ISBN: 978-1-6655-3710-0 (sc)
ISBN: 978-1-6655-3709-4 (hc)
ISBN: 978-1-6655-3711-7 (e)

Print information available on the last page.

Published by AuthorHouse 09/02/2021

authorHOUSE®

DEDICATION

I dedicate this book to all the creatures I have rescued and loved.

And to all the people who protect them.

This book should inspire others to look for pets at rescue groups, Humane Societies and shelters.

There are so many animals in need of forever homes and love.

Zoe is a Pit Bull

She had no idea that some people thought she was a bad dog, a bitey kind of dog that would hurt children.

Someone must have found her but let her loose and she had puppies.

The owners found homes for all of the puppies, but Zoe was sick.

She had lumps on her body - a large one on her left side and smaller ones on her tummy and leg.

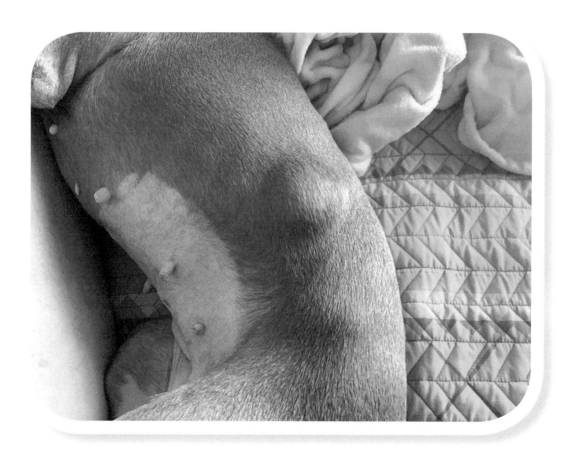

Her owners did not want to keep her and took her to a shelter so maybe someone else would adopt her and help her.

A lady came to look for a dog since one of her dogs died.

She saw Zoe and the big lump. She was worried, but Zoe jumped on her lap and kissed her.

How could anyone not love this dog?

So she was adopted.

Once in her new home, Zoe was happy but, after going to the vet, three lumps were found to be cancer.

Zoe had surgery on the 3 lumps and 8 more that were not cancer.

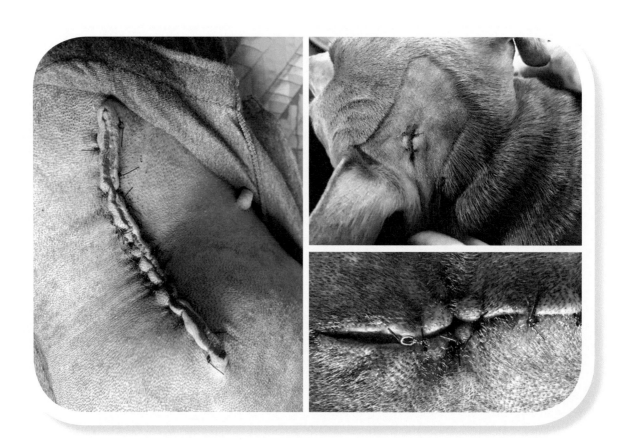

She had to wear cones and doggie jammies for a long time to cover her stitches and keep her from opening up her wounds.

Finally, Zoe was all healed and no longer sick. She was so happy that she zoomed around the house with her toys.

The lady who adopted her took a chance. Zoe would have died without surgery and many people would not want a dog that needed so much help and cost lots of money.

Sometimes, when we are searching for a new pet, we look for the one who is bright eyed and bushy tailed, forgetting the little one in the back that looks sad.

Perhaps that is the one who needs the most help.

Pit Bulls and Rottweilers and some other dogs are called bad but they are not all bad dogs. Giving them love and training will teach them to feel secure, just like some children.

And, maybe, a zoomie dog like Zoe helped the one who adopted her, bringing love where it was needed

Zoe and her new family of dogs and cats were all rescued. So, if you want your own zoomie dog, there's one waiting at a shelter or rescue group. You know where to find them…

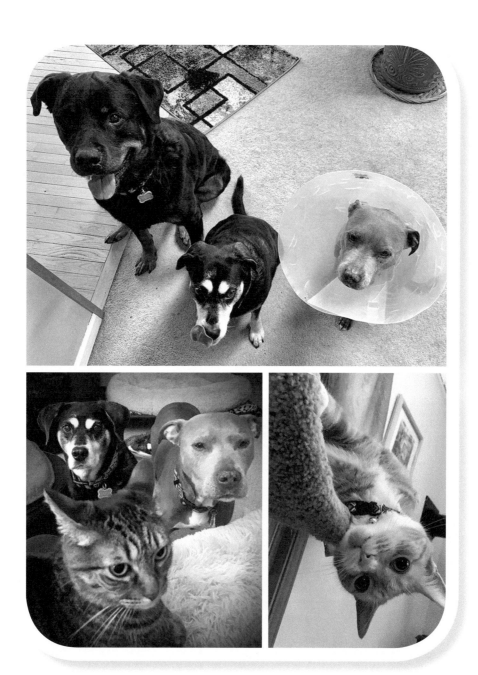

ABOUT THE AUTHOR

Kathy Kuzma is a retired teacher who lives in the country with her husband, two cats and three dogs. Her love of nature is relevant to all aspects of life. After obtaining a bachelor's degree in English from Wayne State University, Kathy went on to receive her master's degree in Special Education from Oakland University. She taught at the secondary level in English and Special Education and became a Teacher Consultant at the elementary level.

Kathy has written 4 books of poetry and one other children's book. They are on Barnes & Noble and Amazon.com. Her pen name is Katje Kaase.

Her two adult children and three grandchildren provide her with endless adventures. Rescuing animals who have been abused or neglected has been a lifetime commitment.

Printed in the United States
by Baker & Taylor Publisher Services